DR DANIELLE E

the dip

A practical guide to take control of screen addiction and reconnect your family.

For parents of teenagers

The Dip: A practical guide to take control of screen addiction and reconnect your family. For parents of teenagers.

First edition

Published by Distinct Psychology

Einstein, Danielle.   9780648575702 (pbk.)

Production credits
Edited by Russell Thomsen and Lauren Finger
Cover Design by Sam Dahl
Photograph by Giselle Haber
Editorial Assistance from Lauren Finger
Printed by Ingram Spark

Author's notes The 'Notes' section at the back of this book contains references to the text and useful additional information on the specific points mentoned in the chapters. Each reference is linked by page number and relates to a particular section of the text.

To all parents struggling right now. I've often wondered about the point of our own career goals if we can't support the mental health of our children. I hope this book will provide you with ideas and renewed energy to build your family!

Danielle Einstein

Sydney, Australia

Contents

Preface

Life has completely transformed in the past decade. Since the rise of the mobile phone, it is has become virtually impossible to switch off from our everyday commitments. Work expectations are never-ending. With 24/7 communication, we parents can't seem to find time in the day anymore for ourselves or our families. Life has simply become too busy and the tech revolution has made it increasingly harder to manage our own devices, as well as those we provide for our children.

First and foremost, it is important to understand that the obsession with technology in our homes and among our children is not our fault. It has been deliberately manipulated in ways that will be discussed in the following chapters. We are not 'bad' parents for sometimes ignoring devices in the hands of our children while we do other things. In fact, many of my friends will find it ironic that I've written this book. After all, my teenage kids' use of screens is by no means angelic and my husband is addicted to his phone!

A few years ago, while focusing on some major health needs with my extended family, I just let my kids free on their devices and gave up what felt like a losing battle. I've written this book, because last year I took control. I campaigned against phone use in schools (this book explains why) and fine-tuned the programs my organisation runs with secondary-school teachers and students. I have had the benefit of hearing from school counsellors and teachers with regard to which ideas stick and which don't. My plan is to share with you the ones that stick.

I've been surprised by the sheer volume of parents struggling with their kids, and their own, phone use. People whom I'd never anticipate as having difficulties have approached me and opened up when I've given a talk on the topics covered here.

So let me start by saying, screen addiction, and the emotional roller coaster that it can create, is all around us. All we can do is try and support our friends, partners and children to cut down screen addiction. The aim of this book is to give you the knowledge and power to do this for yourself and those within your sphere of influence. So many of us are in this mess and, as a result of a constantly advancing tech industry, it is not about to get any easier.

You won't need this book if your kids self-regulate their devices already. If that's the case, you have probably done a pretty good job of instilling the values and boundaries described in chapters 3 and 4. However, if you are feeling that your family is out of control and that devices and screens are your children's top priority, then you may have allowed unfettered access due to a huge range of reasons. If that is the case, then you will need the help of this book.

If you have chosen to follow a policy of severe restriction I support and applaud you. 'The Dip' approach that is described in this book, and in our program, provides an alternative perspective to this, based on a belief that moderation and family values can be cultivated through education and action. 'The Dip' vision is that it is our job as parents, teachers and psychologists to remain in tune with our teenagers and to help them learn about the ways we are manipulated through smart devices. Hand in hand, we can develop effective skills to manage the emotions stirred up by instant communication.

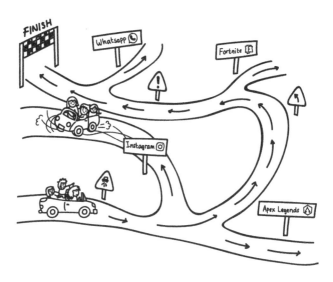

Introduction

HOW TO GUIDE YOUR FAMILY THROUGH THE TECH FRONTIER

I don't think many parents were prepared for the onslaught of problems that smartphones and homework completed on computers has stirred up. As a clinical psychologist and a mother, I feel as if I've woken up in the midst of a racing-car rally. I have a sense of lights flashing in my peripheral vision and feel the whirr of air as cars rush past. I am aware of some cars spinning out of control, while others seem to have found the right balance. Blinking lights warn me of hazards that lie ahead. I often watch members of my family seeking a dopamine hit via their phone to relieve their boredom, frustration or worry (a technology trap known as 'The Dip'). There are times that I feel overwhelmed, though the support and advice of friends and colleagues helps to keep me on track. This book will help you do that too.

The tech revolution has led to a barrage of ways for us to be absorbed, distracted and entertained. This book is intentionally short and sweet. It shows you how to think about screen-time requests, how to shape your family life effectively, and it gives you the means to understand the desire to escape 'The Dip' and other technology traps that lure in children and adults. With some understanding we can see the traps coming and get around them.

Not all device uses are unhealthy, and therein lies the difficulty for parents as they swerve around the racing-car track that they have woken up on. If you take on the challenge of reconfiguring your own device use, it will help you to protect and shape the fabric of your family.

THE WARNINGS

This book has been written because devices are significantly affecting our mood and our brains. In the last year I have found that many of my private practice clients who come to see me for a range of reasons (for example, anxiety, insomnia, depression) now realise that their concerns have been amplified by the destructive effects of smartphone addiction.

For some, adults and children alike, smartphones are leading to a gradual increase in anxiety levels. Research shows that, for the socially isolated, while their online world expands, their offline world and social abilities shrink. Some doctors have used the term 'virtual autism' to describe autistic like symptoms they see for young children with excessive screen time. These disappear once screens are removed. For many children, social skills with people they know well is not the issue; rather, the concern is the lack of incentive and skill to speak with people they know less well, or the abusive and unmanageable behaviour that arises when parents attempt to curb time playing video games.

Recent research has demonstrated a link between screen time and higher instances of depressive symptoms, with social media being particularly harmful. While research within this area is still in its infancy, it has become increasingly clear just how damaging device addiction is; not only to our mental health and that of our kids, but also to our children's quality of learning and their attention spans. Inattention lowers productivity and is yet another documented cost of unlimited connectivity.

While some findings are alarming, on the plus side, smartphones entertain, connect and distract us. They can assist memory, solve problems and allow us to lean on people wherever those people may be. Studies have also shown a decline in depression when devices are used to strengthen and maintain relationships with friends and family.

The mesmerising nature of our phones has altered normal behaviour. At some workplaces it's acceptable to look at a screen rather than the person sitting across a table, or standing on a podium. Headphones cut off people entirely on their way to work or school. It's no surprise that we see people talking on phones while ordering at a restaurant. We've become a phone-corrupted society and basic manners seem to be lost in a void. How have these tiny devices taken such a grip?

According to a survey conducted by Common Sense Media[1], 32 per cent of parents report that they are addicted to their devices. We see television documentaries showing how some families are feeling more divided and despairing than ever before. As smartphones are here to stay, we need to combat our heavy reliance on devices and work out how to take back control. This book is designed to help you to think about small changes that you can make to ensure devices add to, rather than detract from, your family life.

---

1 The leading nonprofit organisation in the US dedicated to improving the lives of kids and families. <https://www.commonsensemedia.org/>

Chapter 1

WHY ARE WE SO ADDICTED IN THE FIRST PLACE?

Neuroscientists think that the happy chemical 'serotonin' kicks into our brain when we feel wanted, important and proud. We temporarily feel great when a friend compliments our latest Instagram post or asks for our advice on WhatsApp messenger.

Dopamine, another significant 'feel good' chemical, is also responsible for giving us a high, and plays an important role in smartphone addiction. Watch a quick video at this link [thedip.com/intro] on how our dopamine levels change in reaction to messages or notifications and create the unstoppable urge to reach and check our phone. 'The Dip' we have spoken of can be understood as the change in dopamine levels shown in the video. It is the downside that follows disappointment; we've looked to our device for a 'hit' and it hasn't been fulfilled. We then crave another pick-me-up and start searching on our phone for any source that might provide it. We get trapped in a vicious cycle of seeking the next small high from our device.

Delta FosB is a regulatory protein that effects the plasticity in our brain. Increasing evidence suggests that Delta FosB collects in a subset of neurons after the use of many kinds of drugs of abuse as well as following compulsive behaviours. When we collect too much Delta FosB, the brain adapts by requiring higher levels of dopamine to achieve the same reward feeling it used to achieve on less. This is one of the ways scientists believe that our brains change and, in the case of Delta FosB, it leads to addictions. There is an argument that teenagers are even more vulnerable to addiction than adults due to poor impulse control and a combination of the neurological changes that result from rewards encountered through device use.

Moving back to a simple explanation, it is not surprising that so many of us are addicted. The moment people you really care about want you, you have a strong internal pull to be there for them; the need to look after others distracts you from whatever you were doing. You get a buzz when they care about you too. If we are waiting for a message, the urge to check our phones is irresistible. Studies show that we have poorer working memory and fluid intelligence (the ability to think logically in new situations without any prior knowledge) when our phone is near.

Since it is so easy to get addicted to our smartphones, it's no wonder that our devices are slowly taking over our lives. The constant buzzing from incoming messages and app notifications create a never-ending stream of distraction by pulling our attention back to the device. We react to boredom, frustration and 'the dip' in our mood by reaching for our phones. Our addiction has become so severe that a specific term, 'nomophobia', was named 2018 Word of the Year by Cambridge Dictionary to describe the stress some people experience when they are without or unable to use their smartphones!

Chapter 2

THE REALITY OF SMARTPHONE AND DEVICE USE: UNDERSTANDING THE FACTORS THAT LURE US IN AND PLAY WITH OUR MOODS

Part A: The value of being connected

As humans, our social standing is enhanced when we are connected with what is happening in the world around us. Devices connect us both with each other and with relevant headlines (news, financial, social, sport, hobby inspired) to keep us up to date. No single person could stay abreast of all culturally helpful information on their own, so seeking out news and information allows us to learn from others and keep in the loop within our community. Quite simply, we are better off when we are switched on and know what is going on.

We also are susceptible to a human desire to be thought about, seen, heard, guided and monitored by others. All these functions are brilliantly served by social media. As parents, we need to understand the powerful pull of such connections on our children and ensure that we are listening, caring for, guiding and monitoring them (not in a helicopter-parent, over the top way). It's hard but we need to give our children enough time and attention individually so that they sense we are interested in them. It won't eliminate their need to fit in with others, but it will help with setting a tone of values, boundaries and screen-time limits. Dr Michael Carr-Gregg, a leader in this area, has suggested that we need to provide eight minutes per day with every child (on their own) giving them the attention they need.

Part B: Getting reassurance for every doubt

Whether it be texting our worries to friends or using Google the moment a question crosses our minds, smartphones provide reassurance for every doubt. Unfortunately, a negative side effect of this instant world is growing impatience, and the undermining of our willingness to wait to find things out.

In unpublished research that we are currently conducting at Macquarie University, we've seen an association between separation anxiety and the rate that teenaged students say their parents text them to know where they are. It's not really a surprise to hear that the more parents text to see if their children have safely arrived somewhere, the more children will report feeling anxious when they are separate from their parents.

In terms of general life problems multiple studies have shown that people who feel desperate to know what the future will bring are more likely to display a greater number of simultaneous psychological difficulties than people with high tolerance for uncertainty. So in our Dip@School program we teach students to increase their patience, lower their catastrophising and reduce their need to control what is about to happen to them (see Step 2, pages 30 to 32 below).

Part C: Proving yourself to be right or interfering with conversation flow

A less than pleasant use of the smartphone is when it is used to prove a point at the dinner table. Some parents find themselves drawn into settling disputes by looking the answer up during a meal. If that is a habit you have gotten into, ask yourself whether it is benefiting your family or bringing out the worst of your personality. Likewise, when a visitor brings out their phone at a dinner party, it stems the flow of conversation. Conversations have the power to bring people together through shared stories, opinions and memories. A phone at the table halts conversation and divides attention amongst those who vie for space to see the screen.

Part D: Envy

Sometimes we feel worse rather than better when scrolling through our social media feeds. The reason we feel so low is due to envy, a feeling known as the 'green-eyed monster' for a good reason. Comparing ourselves to others is useful as it prompts us to consider whether we are meeting our own goals. When a person feels envy, they can either do more to work towards their goal or realise they aren't going to achieve it, and then shift gears and aim for something else. Envy becomes destructive when the person denies it is there. Our research shows that envy is linked to anger, depression and can compromise being productive.

We are most susceptible to becoming envious when scrolling through social media if we follow people who are moving fast towards what we see as our own personal goals or elusive dreams. These might well be ambitions that we have already discarded. Whether they are friends or acquaintances, we are more vulnerable to envy when we know a lot about the person or feel similar to them and then witness them meeting these same goals that we haven't achieved.

Studies have shown that constant social media contact is associated with loneliness and self-confidence issues, with more than three hours of screen time per day being associated with depression and suicidal outcomes. The early research showed that envy among Facebook users was strongly associated with whether individuals experienced depression as a result of its use. We can respond in a healthy way to envy so as to minimise its ability to lower our mood.

Envy no longer has a strong ability to undermine us if we are happy to talk (or indeed laugh) about it with someone we trust. Many people now also exercise self-discipline by de-friending those particular people that they most compare themselves to, or restricting themselves from using particular apps that cause envy for them (Instagram, Snapchat, LinkedIn).

▶ The tips for managing jealousy and envy that I ask parents to use with teenage clients is the **'DIM Envy' (Does It Matter)** method. The steps are set out below:

1. **D**iscuss the feeling and make it seem normal to experience envy or jealousy. The unhealthy loop of comparisons can lead to depression if it isn't recognised.

   - Label envy and encourage your child to confide in you or a close friend of theirs. Sometimes friends will laugh together, and even find out that the friend feels the same way! This releases some of the tension.

2. **I**solate the triggers

   - Understand the pattern of triggers that sets your child off. For example:

     ○ they find out about a party they haven't been invited to via Facebook;

     ○ they see a Snap Map location of their friends together;

     ○ they don't get offered a place on an exchange program; or

     ○ they see an Instagram post of someone with an amazing body.

3. **M**ake a change

- Encourage your child to question whether their desire to have what they are missing, should remain one of their top goals. If it does, then rethink how to get there.

- If they really can't attain that goal, help them alter what they are aiming for. For example, which other friends, sport or interest can they prioritise?

- If their desire isn't one of their top goals, then get used to laughing it off with them, as it's just a trigger.

Also while they pass time (and have to put up with feeling a little cranky) encourage them to:

- ○ Distract with an activity

- ○ Look after a friend/relative/pet

- ○ Disconnect from identified social media triggers for a while.

Chapter 3

HOW TO DEVELOP 'SMART' DEVICE BOUNDARIES FOR YOUR FAMILY

So, as parents, what should we do?

Step One: B.A.T.H. Analysis

For each app that you and your children use, understand the **Benefit** to **Addiction** ratio. Take into account the amount of **Time** typically spent on it and whether the app has a **Healthy** impact on your mood.

BATH = Benefit: Addiction: Time: Healthy impact

The **Benefit** is the degree to which the app helps us achieve one of our set goals for the day.

Addiction refers to the way the app creates highs and lows inside us (think of these as the hit and dip produced by dopamine release as shown in The Dip video). These hits and dips encourage us to stay within the app.

Time is the amount of time that we permit ourselves to use that app.

Healthy impact on our mood. When we turn to our next activity, do we feel energised, sad, cranky or happy?

If we spend too long in the BATH, we get out and our skin is wrinkled. The water is cold and we may not feel rejuvenated. If we spend the right amount of time, we feel clean, refreshed and ready for our next activity. If there is a large addictive element, then take steps to address use of that app (as suggested below). Categorise this for each app. There are two simple categories:

1. Very low rating

The Notes facility on a smartphone has a benefit in providing a memory aid. It has no addictive element. Using this app is unlikely to affect your mood. TripView Lite provides information on public transport (Benefit), it solves a problem and is not addictive. Similar to the Notes app, the TripView Lite app is unlikely to lower your mood (aside from feeling frustrated if there is no easy means of transport nearby).

2. Mid to high rating

The benefits of WhatsApp include being able to message friends and groups through wi-fi plus its general widespread use as a means of communication. It is strongly addictive because of its social nature. One of its features (notifications) increase this addictive grip through repeated dopamine 'hits'. WhatsApp is likely to create 'the dip' if you participate in many large group messages as there is more potential to feel FOMO (fear of missing out), notice negative undertones from a member of a group who you don't get on with or feel annoyed. It also can be difficult to keep up with large group chats (which for teenagers can be non-stop, 500 messages per hour). Setting a time limit on WhatsApp is advisable to ensure restraint.

The benefits of games, such as Ruzzle, are that they keep the player mentally sharp (it uses a timer, and some say it extends their vocabulary). It is addictive, as games are part of a tournament and the player receives points. The game designers want people to continue to play, so the rewards system behind the game has been carefully created to provide 'hits' and 'dips' to keep the player online. It will lower your mood if you binge and use it as an alternative to connecting with people in the room you are in (e.g. your family, if you actually want to connect with them), or completing tasks necessary for the day.

Instagram has benefits in being able to see beautiful photos or keep up with what friends are doing. Its addictive element, the dopamine 'hit', is created by the number of likes that you receive for a post. It has the ability to depress your mood if you are sad and notice feeling the negative effects of envy as many people use it to share their holidays or successes.

Step Two: Recognise if you communicate with others too often, especially when you first have a worry.

The key to learning to cope with less smartphone use can be found in learning to be comfortable with uncertainty. The old saying 'bad news travels fast' is a good guideline. Trust that if something happens to your child or teenager, you will find out pretty fast. Don't respond to the urge to text them because you have a worry cross your mind. Be willing to wait until you hear from them or see them face to face.

Being comfortable with uncertainty improves our ability to cope with worry and makes us less anxious. By realising that we can survive without knowing what is going to happen with small worries, we can tone down the desire to control much of life. This means we adapt when life doesn't go according to plan.

Test yourself

▶   In the absence of information, we jump to the worst conclusions. Try and catch how many times in one day you jump to conclusions when you are unsure of the outcome of situations you consider important.

▶   In the long run, waiting is better! Messaging too early can make it worse and checking too early is a waste of time and can draw your attention from the people you are with. Ask yourself the following questions:

•   Do you check for something you really want before you are likely to hear the answer? For example, your bags don't arrive on a flight and you are told they will let you know once they arrive.

•   Do you set a realistic time frame before you start checking emails etc.?

▶ Answer this question before you reach for your phone: what is a **realistic** time frame? A few hours? A day? A few days? Next week? Next month?

The speed of the internet pushes many of us to be more productive (both workwise or socially). The downside is that, if you tend to be a worrier, it provides more situations for you to try to control or worry about. Teach yourself to ignore the temptation to find out what your friends are doing or how many likes you got on a recent Instagram post. Build up your patience by switching your phone off for a while or deliberately leaving your phone at home. Prioritise the friends or family you have arranged to be with. Our own self-management in dealing with uncertainty is key to helping our children set limits and build resilience.

Step Three: Build Values

Consider what values you want to see in your children, yourself and your community. Respect, cooperative and helpful behaviour, companionship and self-care are the core values that device use seem to undermine.

1. Respect

Do you want your kids to treat others with basic respect? If they are given a drink at a restaurant, should they look up and thank the waiter? Should they pay at a counter while talking on their phone? Should they walk down the street and look to see who is around them? Do you hope they'll greet guests as they enter the house?

These very simple acts are instances that reflect the mindset and actions we seek in our children. I know that for many readers this will be a no-brainer, however, it is easy for even these simple courtesies to slip in the presence of the overwhelming attraction of a device. And because so many parents are time poor and addicted, its these tiny slip-ups that erode the respect our children show to others.

The fact that so many adults act similarly reflects a new type of entitlement. The message given out by any adult who walks while texting on the phone is, 'I must have this conversation now, and I don't care if that means that I might walk into you, walk slowly or fail to smile or make eye contact.' The motivator might be the person being in a rush, pressured or enamoured with the person on the other end of the phone, but nevertheless it shows a basic disrespect for those they share a physical space with.

Caring about the people around you means respecting the fact that they are giving you their time. If you are a person who reaches for your phone in anyone's company, *it silently communicates to the person that you are with that they are not important to you or worth your attention.* You may not intend this but that is its meaning. Over time, that meaning builds up through your non-verbal behaviour and affects every relationship you exhibit it in.

Some may argue that we just need to toughen up and hang out in places where this style of device use is acceptable – it's just the new way of relating in a tech-driven world. Interestingly enough, the annual view of Global Risks released by the World Economic Forum (WEF), based on a survey of 1000 respondents drawn from the Davos community of company chiefs, politicians, civil society and academics stated that one of the most pressing issues is **digital isolation** among stressed-out individuals. When the report was launched in London, Alison Martin, group chief risk officer at Zurich Insurance Group warned, 'The world is sleepwalking into catastrophe.'

2. Cooperative and helpful behaviour

Do you need your children to help you at specific times of the day (e.g. setting the table for dinner, cleaning up after themselves, assisting others when needed, preparing a meal)? Have you found that the presence of a screen means the answer that you get is either a 'yes', followed by no action, or 'in a minute', followed by five further requests and a rage from you or your child?

This basic and common expectation is being disrupted by devices. Of course, chores are not going to appeal to a 14-year-old and there have been many times that I have let them slip in our home. I'm often exhausted and it's easier to do the chore myself than pester my sons. However, we dig ourselves into a major 'let screens interfere with them contributing chores to the house' hole. Recall that a screen's addictive hold over an individual is similar to that which we would experience in the midst of an exciting movie at the cinema.

3. Providing you with companionship

My children have reacted fairly responsively when I've told them I need some time with them or that I feel lonely when they are constantly in their own world with eyes glued to a screen with earphones blocking any communication. They seem more willing to engage in conversations around the dinner table. They are generally more chatty and, as a result, their ability to interact with others generally is improving,

4. Self-care

The two self-care factors undermined by limitless device use are sleep and body image. Both are topics to discuss at home.

Sleep

We are naturally wired to wake up for rewards, be they social (believing an exciting message awaits) or a game (e.g. Fortnite or Apex Legends). The sense of being drowsy, which we need to notice and listen to, is also disrupted by the same factors. So, in order to protect ourselves from impact on our sleep, we need to have a pattern whereby we switch off communication and social media aspects of devices around an hour before bed. Similarly, in the mornings, we need to set a time before which our children are not allowed to play games (otherwise they may wake themselves up to play). Unchecked, that time may become earlier and earlier.

Body Image

Ensure you have reminded your children that amazing photos are manipulated. If you need some assistance in this discussion, there is a great snippet from BTN(https://ab.co/2ERkczs) which will help with this discussion.

Chapter 4

WHY SHOULD WE DEVELOP OUR OWN BOUNDARIES?

The current recommendation by the <u>Office of the E-safety Commissioner (https://bit.ly/2WH0wIx)</u> for children between the ages of 5 and 17 years is less than two hours per day for non-educational use. Two US surveys based on 506,820 teenagers indicated that those who spent more time on social media and smartphones were more likely to report mental health issues (in particular, depressive symptoms) than those who spent more time on non-screen activities. In that research paper the concerning risks were described as 'constant social media use' and 'over 3 hours' per day reported on screens.

However, underneath it all, parents need to guide balanced use of technology. It's really the addictive nature of games, entertainment and messaging (as set out in the BATH analysis) that we need to train our children to manage.

A sensible aim is that *at times* all members of the family can:

a) calm themselves without a screen

b) occupy themselves without a screen

c) participate in extra school activities (leading to less time available that day)

d) find it easy to put the family first (for discrete time periods) and

e) respect the values described in Chapter 3 (respect, cooperative and helpful behaviour, providing you with companionship and self-care).

Time limits are a useful way to help children achieve all of this when they otherwise seem to have lost their capacity to reach them independently. Children are often willing to consider how to devise a system together that helps them keep to a healthy limit.

Children copy the behaviour of their parents, so acknowledging our own addiction is a starting point. If you spend an extended amount of time on your own device, chances are your kids recognise the occupied expression on your face and translate this to freedom from their own smartphone limits. This has recently become such an issue that we often hear of some kids putting screen-time limits on their own parents!

The fact is, many parents need to use their phones for work. However, just checking a device has the power to immediately place a work demand at the front and centre of your focus. So consider how to place screen-time limits on yourself (e.g. set downtime or put your phone away for 30 mins when you get home from work, first thing in the morning and during meals, consider not looking at your phone just because you hear the bell announcing that a message has arrived). Learn to check your phone when it suits you, rather than the moment someone wants you.

Chapter 5

OK, SO HOW DO I PUT THIS INTO PRACTICE?

SETTING BOUNDARIES: WHERE TO START

Before you sit down with your family:

- **Ensure** your partner is supportive of your initiative. You might ask them to read this book!

- **Decide** how much screen use is automatic during the school term (see FAQ Question 1).

- **Decide** which devices will be permitted and which will be banned during the school week (e.g. some families choose to exclude all Xbox/Playstation use mid-week).

- **Invest** in understanding your child's current favourite apps/
  games. Take an interest and be excited about how those apps/
  games work. Don't dismiss them or be judgemental. This
  will help your child realise that you are not against the app/
  game, which may be important to their lives (see connecting
  purpose described above), but rather that your aim is to
  contain the time-consuming or disruptive nature of it for
  your family life.

  ▶ Play a video game together and make an effort to learn a
    bit about what interests your child about the game – let
    them discuss it with you. For example, if they like to
    copy the dance moves from the Fortnite game, ask them
    about the purpose of the dance moves and when they
    use them in the game, or why, when they are playing,
    do they make their character laugh?

Spend time separately with each child:

- Discuss which screen uses you wish to permanently allow that
  will not be subject to the time limit.

  ▶ For example, a child may wish to have their Notes
    available all the time, or an app such as the TripViewLite
    or Moovit app (which provide public transport infor-
    mation). For this purpose, consider the BATH analysis

explained above. Also base this decision on the screen-time report that their device provides.

- Understand their reasons for accessing specific functions across their devices. Each child will have different uses and priorities. Find out which are essential and which are desired. This will help your child consider how to allocate their daily allowance and will keep them on board with the process. In a few days' time, specify time limits per individual app. The instructions for this are in Chapter 6.

  ▶ For example, one teenage client explained that he wanted to watch three YouTube gamers on his computer every day. Two gamers post a 10-minute clip, while one posted a 15-minute clip. He explained how this helps him play and keep in line with his friends. Together there was an agreement that the two-hour screen-time limit would therefore incorporate the 35 minutes of YouTube. His mum agreed to this, and therefore set a 35-minute daily limit on YouTube.

- Some teenagers who have experienced depression or bullying may choose not to participate in certain social media activities. One teenage client told me that she had chosen to only use WhatsApp for direct messaging. She used it for one specific group of friends who she played netball with as they used it to make plans, but she no longer participated in other group chats.

When you sit down as a family:

Find a time that suits family members to talk, don't just spontaneously launch in because YOU have the time and are in the mood to get started! Teenagers are more collaborative when they feel they've been invited. During the discussion, choose the ideas that you wish to experiment with. Some of the ideas here will fit for your family, some won't. Think of it as a three-week long experiment which you will tinker with and adjust as necessary.

Mention the reasons that you are putting this in place. Discuss both your fears about unchecked screen use (described in the FAQ Question 6) and also wanting to be part of a family that upholds and respects the values described in Chapter 3.

- Decide on media-free 'unplugged' locations within the house e.g. dining room, bathroom.

- Agree that there will be no screens used during family meal times. This means no turning to devices to answer questions at the dinner table.

- If you expect chores to be completed each day, discuss how to make wi-fi or device use dependent on the chores being completed. Some families have found that they have to change their wi-fi password every day while the new house rule is being set up. They provide the new wi-fi password after chores are finished. Cyber safety software such as Family Zone and Apple Screentime, provide a different option for navigating this, as wi-fi use can be switched off from the parents' phone by using the sleep button. This should only be needed during the set up phase.

- Introduce the understanding that there will be blocks of screen-free time on weekends (between 45 minutes and two hours) for all family members. Decide on this time frame based on your family's standard media consumption[2]. Smartphones/laptops/iPads/TVs etc. are to be switched off during this time.

---

2 According to a 2013 US survey some families are media centric, spending an average of 11 hours per day on screen media at home (computers, tv and smartphones). Other families are media moderate, spending an average of 4.5 hours per day on screen media at home and other families are media light, spending fewer than 2 hours per day with screen media.

- Insist that they are ready on time for family activities. If they know you are all going out, then they need to allow themselves enough time to get ready and not be in the midst of a game when it is time to leave. You should not feel obliged to wait for them to finish a game, rather they need to make their playing fit with family arrangements. If there is a dispute, they lose their allocated time for the next day. This simple threat, when it is consistently carried through, will work wonders!

- Remember your child is likely to use up their screen-time allowance the moment they have access to it. That is the nature of addiction. We are drawn to spend as much time as possible, as soon as possible using those apps that have a magical pull on our psyche (as described previously). For example, I asked my son the other day if he would come with me to visit my father in hospital. His answer was yes because he had already used up his phone limit! Without realising it, he implied that, 'I don't have access to anything else right now, so I'm happy to be helpful.'!

- Talk about the fact that there will be occasions when no screen time will be available. Days might occur because of a regular extracurricular commitment, a special event that has come up or because of the busy-ness of everyday life. The aim is for your child to be flexible and be able to skip days when they are sprung on them. Missed screen time on these days does not get saved for subsequent use.

- If multiple devices are used at once (for example, your child is playing a game on a phone whilst watching a movie on an ipad), explain that double screen-time will be used up. Most screentime controls will calculate the time separately, so this is simple to implement. Your kids are learning to control their attention and switch off from the urge for a 'hit'. Research shows that although comprehension is not impaired, recall is poorer from multitasking. The aim is for our kids to control their desire for multiple 'hits'. It builds up the Delta FosB (explained in Chapter One) and has the potential to become a bad habit.

- Some families adopt an open phone policy where the same pass-code is shared between family members, but not open to friends. If you do choose to try this out, respect your children's privacy and do not be tempted to be intrusive. As kids mature, they lean on their friends emotionally, which is healthy. This may also backfire as it is simple for them to get into a habit of deleting messages as they go, which renders checking impossible.

Ways to reduce boredom

- Talk to your kids about having a repertoire of ways to reduce boredom or handle frustration. I call it 'non-screen activity that involves effort'. These are ways to relax that are not social and not pure entertainment (e.g. binge watching YouTube or *Brooklyn 99* on Netflix). If needed, use the Toolbox (page 83) to prompt a discussion.

- Take a moment to consider whether to reward your child with extra screen time. This will remove the natural reward experienced in the task you are trying to encourage. For example, some parents let their kids earn screen time for reading. They may have a ratio, such as for every hour of pleasure reading the children do, they are allowed half an hour of extra media time on the weekend. While this sends a message that reading is valued more than electronic-media time, it alters the motivation to read. Instead of building up a love of reading, your child will view reading as a 'task' and be less likely to persist.

- Talk about the types of motivation that different activities have within them. Intrinsic motivation is the joy that we derive from doing a task when we are fully engrossed in it. For example, being lost in a piece of music or feeling the exhilaration of catching a wave at the beach. Extrinsic motivation is the desire to complete a task because of an external reward that we receive at the end. For example, being paid or earning screen time.

For the first few days:

- Place specific screen-time limits on all devices in each child's possession. This needs to be based on the verbal agreement you have come to.

Monitoring a daily screen-time allowance:

- Realise that you will need to strictly monitor the screen-time limit for a few days. You won't need to keep this up for long, it is just as you establish the system. Once your child reaches their screen limit (across devices) let them know. You are the leader of this new family plan, and the restrictions you have agreed on together need to be respected.

- If you have managed to find an app that will collect a cumulative time limit across devices, fantastic, please let me know! I haven't found one yet. You can now check screen time on phones, computers, PlayStations (as set out in

Chapter 6). If you believe your child has been on a device for a period, your view is what matters. Show some willingness to look at the internet history or write a note regarding their approximate starting time (so that you come across as reasonable). Let them know it is your perception of their time that matters (not the actual time). You should keep up a firm attitude in your discussions.

- Prepare yourself for their frustration. When your kids reach their screen limit for the day (according to the deal you have made) stand your ground and walk away from the ensuing bad behaviour (if you get it). Leave the house if necessary. Remember, that it is also healthy for kids to experience frustration in order to learn how to calm themselves down. Clinical Psychologist Dr Judith Locke explains how many children (she calls them 'Bonsai children') have their lives carefully cultivated to avoid frustration by their parents. This comes at the expense of them building personal resilience.

- Keep a flip phone in the house. If you need to remove all devices but still believe your child requires access to a phone, they can use that the following day. Be prepared to back up your limits day by day. After a few days of your child realising you are serious and that you have a simple but consistent system, they will start to respect the boundaries.

- If you notice long absences in the bathroom (and suspect your child has taken their phone in) confiscate it for the rest of that day. Remember, the consequence of finding this limit has been broken needs to hurt a little, so don't return it after an hour. If there is any doubt when your child is in the bathroom, use 'find my device' on your own phone to set off a tone on your child's handset. You'll only need to do this a couple of times, before they assiduously adopt the new home limit.

- Get really excited when they contain their screen use and respect family expectations. Notice the change they have made. Don't go over the top, but do recognise it with a simple sentence, for example:

  - 'I'm so pleased you switched off your phone the moment I reminded you we had to leave', or

  - 'Well done for dying in the Fortnite game so we could get out the door.' or

  - 'Thanks for being helpful tonight. I really appreciated how quick you were to finish the game.'

- Remember that children also communicate with their friends for emotional support using their devices. Do not take devices away for weeks at a time. You may need to limit use for the rest of a day or a subsequent day, but keep it at that. Consistency is the key here.

Suggestions for the morning and evening:

- Limit screens first thing in the morning. Spend time waking up, connect with each other, even if it is only for a few minutes. Mornings are a busy time, with parents preoccupied, so try not to leave your child with 30 minutes of their favourite YouTuber, TV series, or gamer over their breakfast cereal. Keep screens for kids (aged up to 14 years) to 15 minutes, they may need to check emails to get organised for school. Family Zone has a good option for devising specific device use limits for times of day (e.g. from 7.15 to 8.30am you may select the study option and only have news websites, emails and educational resources available; ensure there is no access to youtube at that time of day). If your child does zone out with a screen in the morning, remind them that it is consuming their daily limit.

- At night time, all phones go to a central phone charging station. Check that computers are off, if you find this is not happening then shut down the home wi-fi and move computers out of bedrooms.

  ▶ Sometimes a phone is needed in the bedroom for an alarm to wake up in the morning. The simplest way to resolve this is to purchase a cheap alarm clock for every bedroom.

Build Alternative Activities:

- If your house has become intricately associated with screen use, get out of the house together and leave phones at home or in the car. This prevents the habit of constantly checking your devices while participating in a family activity.

We enjoy watching some television at home and being able to share the experience is nice for our family. Choosing a show involves some compromise. If one family member doesn't agree with the choice, that's fine, they don't need to join the family. However they cannot go and watch their own show on a separate device unless it is within their allocated screen-time limit for the day. Communal television watching is not part of our daily screen allowance.

Have you caught yourself, your partner or your child playing a game, or chatting with other friends, while watching a show with you? (AKA splitting their attention). I feel that this undermines the point of family time, as it means that person still isn't giving the family their undivided time. If my kids are on their phones while we are watching a show together I ask them to put their phone in another room. This removes the temptation to use it. The only way for family screen time to be excluded from the agreed allowance is for all those watching to have their attention on that show.

- Simply saying, 'Find something else to do' never works. The key is to back up your rhetoric with activities that either get you all off screens together or promote shared engagement as a family.

- Show your children that you prioritise them above others in your network. Participate in activities together. Here are some that might appeal. Ironically, some of these will use a screen.

  o Walk the dog to a new location, play with the dog, make it fun and leave your phone at home, reinforce your children by being playful.

  o Play a card game or a board game. My kids love poker, 500, and a charade game (which uses a phone). If you do this regularly as a family, you might observe them teaching these games to other family friends and, bizarrely, even those children may leave their phones for a while.

  o Listen to music or a podcast together.

  o Cook a meal or bake a cake.

  o Watch a TED talk or documentary on YouTube or Netflix to learn something new.

- ○ Come up with an idea that will lead to a donation to a charity.

- Talk to your child about the importance of building strengths. These are shown by developing an interest in an activity (such as sport, IT, drama, music, art). They foster internal qualities such as perseverance, curiosity and courage. If your child can find activities that reflect their strengths, they will be good at the chosen activities and the activities will leave your child feeling stimulated. Talk about creative tasks too. Creative tasks distract us from worries, build confidence and provide space to work through problems encountered in everyday life. At some point most teenagers will wish to get a job or apply for an opportunity offered at school. At that time, being able to show that there are a range of activities that they have participated in outside home, and hobbies that they pursue at home, will improve their chance of being selected.

- If you are going out with another family, text a parent ahead and suggest phones are left in the car. Keep a deck of cards handy.

During school holidays:

- Reset the screen time limits so that computer and gaming consoles can only be accessed after a nominated time in the afternoon (e.g. 3 pm).

- Chat with them about their plans. Let your child know that a little more is expected of them around the house. Set aside a work task that you can pay them for, or if they are over 14 years, encourage them to look for a job at the local shops.

- Agree that they can have 3 hours instead of 2 hours (although make the additional hour one that needs to be earnt) with 'non-stimulating' activities around the house.

- Agree that random days will be Xbox or movie free. On these days, other activities will take over. When they occur, you expect your child to show the maturity to roll with the complete lack of screen time.

- If your child struggles with disconnecting from screens and engaging one to one, consider taking a wi-fi-free holiday with your kids to help remind them how much fun they can have without a device.

Tips for gaming consoles:

Xbox/PlayStation

▶ I recommend a strong approach to Xbox and PlayStation use due to the huge number of behavioural difficulties that emerge when children are allowed unfettered access. It's not a surprise, the social side of gaming consoles means that your child may feel like they are attending a very cool party in the comfort of your home. This occurs whenever there are a lot of people playing online or they are hitting new 'tiers' or 'targets'.

▶ If you haven't started like this, and now want to introduce a change, make sure you engage with your child and understand why they love the games and what its significance is for them. Use the last five minutes of Xbox/PlayStation time to talk about what they need to do to get to the next tier of the game.

Once you have bonded with your child over the game, you can then follow the previous steps about general screen-time use. Introduce Gaming Console control once you have a working relationship based on the family values you are speaking about and the BATH analysis.

There are a few ways to manage Xboxes:

- Some families decide to ban the Xbox or PlayStation during the week. While children complain of 'social suicide', the approach provides very firm boundaries that teenagers respond well to after their initial complaints. It completely eliminates fighting between siblings and attempts to haggle with parents. The social suicide does not eventuate.

- Others limit use to one hour per day. Again this is met with disdain initially but once the parental controls have been set and parents remain firm devilish behaviour disappears.

A comment on Smart Watches

The Dip video shows how easily we get pulled in to check our device through notifications. We also get pulled in by physically seeing a device. Much of the advice on screen-time control suggests putting a phone in a bag, on a charger, leaving it in the car or placing it out of sight and out of reach. Smart watches are not designed to be taken off. We are more likely to lose them if they are not being worn. The reminder sitting on our wrist is constant, as is the unconscious pull to check. Please read the article I wrote in 2017 about how phones may increase anxiety levels, and the importance of sitting with 'not knowing' to understand the reasons I discourage smart watches.

Tips for Computers:

The last stumbling block is the humble computer. The computer can enrich learning. Without restrictions, it can also transport focus far away from lessons. Self-regulation is the goal we aim for with computer use (as with all device use). The same websites, apps and other distractions as accessed by phones and PlayStations can be mirrored on the computer by our skilled children. With BYOD embraced across many schools, students use their own computers during the day and then again, after school for their homework. The good news is if you have started to take a firm stance on the screen-time changes for phones and gaming consoles, the behaviour you are shaping is more easily transferred across to computer use.

Placing limits on a computer is a horrendous nightmare but I still recommend several attempts. I failed abysmally when I started. I placed the normal Family Zone parental limits on one of my children's computers. There were several days of complaints that he was locked out during French, History and other subjects (although, to be honest, he probably liked the excuse of not having to complete the classwork). Despite the school having purchased Family Zone, it seemed as though the teachers did not assist sufficiently, as they suggested new websites to access in class that were not approved by their own IT department. Another option is for schools to provide devices which have severe restrictions placed on them for use in specific classes. I think parents need to petition schools to take Family Zone and other computer options seriously.

Microsoft offers excellent parental controls on their computer software. Their controls allow parents to set a time limit per day, permitted hours of use, and to differentiate across days of the week. It automatically emails parents screen time used by each child through a weekly activity report. This is extremely useful for setting limits. At this point in time Family Zone does not offer this facility. Depending on your children's age and their school's usage policy, you can fairly sensibly set an upper limit. At the very least, your child will let you know if they constantly need more time. You can then discuss how to adjust the system. The aim is to transfer the onus of responsible screen use to our kids. This occurs when they realise they have to allocate their time limits sensibly.

EXPECT RESULTS

Keep in mind that kids are clever with technology and can figure out how to circumnavigate the boundaries set on their phones by apps and phone software! Agreed family screen-time boundaries are the best way to combat excessive device use.

▶ It's amazing how the kids respond and self-regulate when they realise limits will be imposed. They do prioritise which types of use they desperately want within the day, and which types they can cut down. They also seem to be more pleasant to be with as there aren't constant undertones of a battle.

▶ If you and your kids use Apple devices, use the Screen Time Report to help encourage a balance. It is a fantastic development with the potential to really enact change if you put in a few days of effort into it with your kids. Look closely at the number of pick ups (and the time of day that they tend to occur). Ask them how they manage their notifications when they are trying to study or spend time with friends. Also look at the overall time spent each day. Chapter 6 describes how to discuss the screen time report and handle requests for more time.

▶ Finally, give yourself some encouragement for doing this now! Ask yourself whether, as a parent, you feel that these limits need only be imposed during pressured times (e.g. the final year of school year), or should you be aware of helping your children curb addictions before these times hit? As you can tell, my leaning is the latter.

WRAP UP

For me, a combination of Microsoft Windows and Apple Screen Time works the best. Both permit me to see cumulative time that has been used. As one of my children has used a Microsoft Windows based computer and the other has an Apple computer, I've been able to compare them. The Microsoft Windows parental controls are more useful than the apple version because they track the amount of time actually spent on the computer per day and feed that back to parents via automated emails.

The benefit of Family Zone, is that it allows an instant way of switching off online use with one tap. You can also use Apple Downtime to remove wi-fi access to an IPhone, it's just a little more fiddly.

The final alternative remains just taking devices away. I've found that, over time, just bringing attention to the use of screens has led to an improvement across our device use. It's allowed me to remind my kids about values and they really understand the impact of their device use on the family feeling, in the end they seem to be more respectful. It hasn't been an easy run and it's still not perfect but we are in a better state than ever!

Chapter 6

STEP-BY-STEP GUIDE
TO SCREEN-TIME CONTROLS

In 2018 Apple software (iOS 12) introduced a Screen Time function where users can see how much time they have spent on their phone/iPad etc. and specific apps, as well as set limits for their device usage.

APPLE DEVICES: IPHONE, IPAD ETC.

1. Navigate to **Settings** → **Screen Time** (1.1) When you open Screen Time for the first time, you can specify if you are a parent setting up an account for a child. Then you can set up a parent passcode that will be required to alter Screen Time settings. If your family uses Family Sharing across Apple devices, you can also select 'Set Up Screen Time for Family' (1.2) to access your child's Screen Time reports and set controls from your own device.

1.1

1.2

2. Click on the **Screen Time Report** (2.1) which will expand
   into a bar graph that shows you how much time you have
   spent on your phone in a day or week (2.2). From here, you
   can see a breakdown of the time spent on specific apps (2.3),
   as well as view how many times you pick up your phone in
   an hour (2.4).

   ▶   Discuss the Screen Time Report with your kids and
       identify the main unhealthy habits – whether this be
       many hours spent on a social media app (e.g. Instagram,
       WhatsApp, or others) or excessive time spent on YouTube.

2.1

2.2

2.3

2.4

3.1

3.2

3.3

3.4

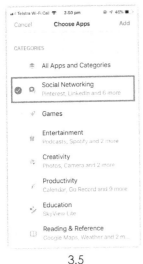

3.5   3.6

3. You can set a limit on an individual app by going to
   your **Screen Time Report** (see 2.1), tapping the bar
   graph (see 2.2), and then scrolling down to see your **Most
   Used** apps (see 2.3). Select the app (e.g. '**Instagram**') scroll
   down and select **Add Limit** (3.1) then select appropriate time
   limit using the **Time** toggle (3.2) Make sure to select **Block
   at End of Limit.**

   ▶   A good rule of thumb is to limit a particular app to half
       an hour (see 3.2), and also to limit time spent across
       ALL Social Networking apps to 1 hour and 15 minutes.
       To do this, go to **App Limits** (3.3) → **Add Limit** (3.4)

→ **Social Networking** (3.5) and select appropriate time limit using **Time** toggle (3.6) Make sure to select **Block at End of Limit.**

▶ If your child wants more time on a particular day and you can see that their device use is really in control (i.e. they are respecting family values and do not seem to be preoccupied with their phones), then you may wish to sit down and have a proper discussion about extending their permissions to 1½ hours per day. Remember that the daily screen-time limit recommended in Australia is two hours – this means that the **maximum** social media allowed for any child should be two hours per day.

4. If Screen Time for Family is enabled, you will also receive a notification to approve extra screen time on your phone from their device, if your child requests more time when a time limit has expired. (Of course, they will!) Be wary of being so busy that you just accept every request that is asked of you. **A sensible habit is to accept two 15-minute extensions (rather than the hour extensions) and then no more**. If you have a few days of extending hour upon hour and letting go of the limits, then sit down and look at the Screen Time Report again and talk to your child.

▶ Within these discussions, acknowledge that there are times that you are busy and are not a perfect parent. In those times, you are 'weaker' and might slip up, by permitting too many extensions.

▶ The process of developing screen-time limits based on values means that you'll be limiting it to a half an hour extension and are willing to review screen use together if you don't feel that you have a working family balance.

5. Review precise app limits based on the Screen Time Report (Step 3). This is possible and doesn't take long once you get the hang of it.

▶ For an instructional video on how to set up Screen Time on an Apple device, <u>click here</u>.(https://bit.ly/2KPyli9).

▶ For an instructional video on how to set up Screen Time for your child using your own device, <u>click here</u>. (https://bit.ly/2WpxTAj) Note: Family Sharing must be enabled.

ANDROID

For Android devices (Samsung, Sony, Nexus, HTC One, Google Pixel etc.), many screen time apps, such as Boomerang and Screen-time are available for download on the Google Play store.

If you create a Google Account for your child using Family Link, you can install screen-time limits on a device. Once you set up a limit, your child will receive a notification if their device is about to be locked. They are still able to answer the phone and use the Emergency Call button providing the device has a telephone plan.

In order to set this up:

1. Open the **Family Link** app.

2. Select your child.

3. On the '**Daily Limit**' card, tap **Set Up** or **Edit Limits**.

4. Follow the instructions on the screen to set daily limits.

▶ Daily limits apply to each Android device or Chrome-book your child uses. For example, if you set a daily limit of two hours, your child would get two hours of time on each device. If your child has more than one device, set a lower limit based on their normal tendencies.

Lock/unlock your child's Android device:

1. Open the **Family Link** app.

2. Select your child.

3. On the card for one of your child's Android devices, tap **Lock Now** or **Unlock**.

▶ You can use a parent passcode to unlock your child's Android device if it isn't connected to the Internet.

GAMING CONSOLES

▶ For instructional videos on how to set limits on gaming consoles, click here.(https://bit.ly/319qHqD)

▶   Play Station 4 has the advantage of allowing parents to limit the amount of time played per day for each child. Set up a family member account and then open <u>Play Time Controls,</u> (<u>https://bit.ly/3172lhy</u>) which can be found under Settings >Parental Controls>Family Management. Play Time settings will permit you to apply these limits. They can be set using a web browser, on the actual PS4 or via the app.

▶   The Family Zone box provides a different option for controlling gaming consoles remotely, as long as they use wi-fi (rather than cable). Right now, it doesn't record cumulative time so, as a parent, you need to be aware of when use has started in order to finish it. This is a major limitation in their system.

▶   The final option to monitor a gaming console is to remove the controls. Only provide controls for a specific amount of time. Don't worry about being 'fair', just make a strict rule that the time starts when the controller leaves your hands and finishes when they are placed back. This often means that a gaming console can only be played when you are in the house. The upside of this approach is that your child won't pester you to go out!

COMPUTERS

For links to Apple (https://apple.co/2wAQomf) and
Microsoft (https://bit.ly/2JP1mxm) parental control instructions click here. The following link provides information for
setting parental controls (https://bit.ly/2HAb1Cd) for earlier
editions of Microsoft Windows.

The research suggests that expanded BYOD computer use
in K to 12 classrooms does not add to student results. In
fact, in class computer use lowered undergraduate university
student results between 0.14 to 0.37 points out of a four
point scale. In schools the greater detrimental effect appears
to be for lower performing boys. The natural explanation
to this is twofold: 1) the amount of distraction 2) less
encoding may take place when students type as opposed
to writing. When students write they need to consider the
most important point in a sentence which helps memory,
so writing more because a student has a computer does not
translate into remembering more of the lesson later.

https://www.educationnext.org/should-professors-ban-
laptops-classroom-computer-use-affects-student-learning-
study/

Summary of FAQs

Question 1	How much automatic free screen use is fine?
Dimension to consider	Amount
Rationale	Up to 2 hours per day (is the Australian recommendation). This is based on international research suggesting that too much screen use is associated with a rise in depression, suicidal outcomes, and anxiety which can hit our kids seemingly out of the blue if they haven't developed other strategies to manage their emotions.
Dr Einstein's recommendation	Between 1 and 2 hours. This can increase in the school holidays to 3 hours starting from 3 pm if your child shows initiative through other activities (see Building Alternative Activities page 53)
Difficulty level to implement	Pretty difficult initially, but once the principles have been discussed (based on the values and traps described here). It's achievable!

Question 2	When or where can parents insist on time without screens or earphones?
Dr Einstein's recommendation	Meal times; before school, specific rooms (e.g. bathrooms, dining rooms, car trips).

Question 3	How do families then have shared screen time?
	This is my favourite element of the plan. All of a sudden, siblings have reasons to watch together when parents are out!
Dr Einstein's recommendation	Families can specify that shared screen time in the home is not included in the daily screen-time limit, as long as everyone involved is not using a second device at the time.

Question 4	How do we know which types of screen use are healthy and what limits to place on them?
Dr Einstein's recommendation	Use the BATH analysis. Then look at the screen-time reports to check up every so often.

Question 5	How do parents alter their screen use?
Dr Einstein's recommendation	Watch for the traps that have been described (getting reassurance for every doubt, wanting to connect to others outside the family at the expense of your own family), proving yourself to be right. (pages 21 to 22)

Question 6	What are the problems with unlimited screen use?
Dr Einstein's recommendation	If a child is socially anxious, they are likely to avoid building their 'in person' social skills in preference to easy relationships online. This will get worse. Reduced working memory and fluid intelligence when our phones are near (due to pull of the device). Need for constant external stimulation and difficulties regulating feelings when offline. Reduction in basic manners and in respect shown to others. Difficulties with patience and sitting with uncertainty – this in itself can lead to greater anxiety in those people that are prone to anxiety (click here). <https://bit.ly/2yVowf7>

Question 7	We are implementing the system but my child just ignores it when it doesn't suit them?
Dr Einstein's recommendation	If you feel that your child is ignoring responsibilities (e.g. school activities or family activities), keep implementing the simple consequence. Once the time has elapsed, return to the fact that now they will miss the subsequent day's screen time altogether. Remove all controls and equipment for the next day. Keep at this, over several weeks of calmly placing the same consequence, your child will start to think ahead.

Toolbox

Soothing Through Senses	What ideas do you have for this?	What satisfaction do you feel after trying it? (0 none- 10 heaps)
Sight	E.g. a view, photos of nice holidays you've enjoyed, sunset, stars	E.g. 3
Sound		
Touch		
Taste		
Feel		
Connect		
Care for another person (kindness)		
Look after an animal		

Distract		
Read		
Music		
Exercise		
Getting out of the house		
Help with a meal		
Try a new creative task (prepare a photo album, sketch, write, trial a craft…)		

Notes:

WHICH IDEAS HAVE YOU DECIDED TO TRIAL AT HOME?

Remember:

- Not all ideas need to be taken up

- Be kind to yourself as a parent, you will have good days and bad days in implementing the new routine

- Keep coming back to the new regime whenever you have the energy!

Note more helpful ideas to try...

Note more helpful ideas to try...

AUTHOR NOTES

Introduction

Page 12: **For some, adults and children alike, smartphones are leading to a gradual increase in anxiety levels.** For an in depth explanation of how the overuse of smartphones leads to an increase in anxiety see the following article (Q reader link below).

Einstein, DA (2017) Anxiety and uncertainty in the age of the smartphone — and what we can do about it. The Conversation.  **https://theconversation.com/constantly-texting-your-friends-about-problems-may-be-increasing-your-anxiety-83960**

In a 2017 systematic review, 8 out of 9 studies which included measures of anxiety showed that anxiety was significantly associated with problematic smartphone use. Elhai, JD, Levine, JC, Dvorak, RD, & Hall, BJ (2017). Non-social features of smartphone use are most related to depression, anxiety and problematic smartphone use. *Computers in Human Behavior, 69, 75–82.* In a 2018 meta-analytic review, the same relationship was observed, however in this review, the authors also noticed that the relationship between smartphone use and anxiety strengthened over the 10 years in which studies were published. Vahedi, Z, & Saiphoo, A (2018). The association between smartphone use, stress, and anxiety: A meta-analytic review. *Stress And Health, 34(3),* 347–358. doi: 10.1002/smi. Irrespective of the direction of causation, for those who use their smartphones in the way described, smartphone use will amplify anxiety.

Page 12: **Research shows that, for the socially isolated, while their online world expands, their offline world and social abilities shrink.** Ihm, J (2018). Social implications of children's smartphone addiction: The role of support networks and social engagement. *Journal of behavioral addictions,* 1–9.

A decline in social skills is also becoming more apparent among young children... https://www.madinamerica.com/2017/08/virtual-autism-explain-rising-asd-diagnoses/

Page 13: **Not only to our mental health and that of our kids ...** In another study, those using screens for more than 4 hours a day had lower well-being outcomes than those who used screens for up to 1 hour a day, with more than 7 hours of screen time doubling the risk for lower well-being. The differences for 14 to 17 year olds in this study, were that high users were observed to be less likely to stay calm, tended not to finish tasks, were not curious and argued too much. Twenge, J., & Campbell, W. (2018). 'Associations between screen time and lower psychological well-being among children and adolescents: Evidence from a population-based study.' *Preventive Medicine Reports, 12,* 271-283. doi: 10.1016/j.pmedr.2018.10.003

Page 13: **Recent research has demonstrated a link between screen time and higher instances of depressive symptoms, with social media being particularly harmful.** Research has found that for adolescents the amount of screen time per day – regardless of what the content is – goes hand in hand with the higher instances of depressive symptoms and suicide-related outcomes (including feeling sad/hopeless, considering suicide, planning and attempting to commit suicide) for females, and suicide deaths for males. The study used a cut off of 3 or more hours a day, compared to those using devices for 2 or fewer hours a day. Twenge, JM, Joiner, TE, Rogers, ML, & Martin, GN (2018). Increases in Depressive Symptoms, Suicide-Related Outcomes, and Suicide Rates Among U.S. Adolescents After 2010 and Links to Increased

New Media Screen Time. *Clinical Psychological Science, 6(1),* 3–17. https://doi.org/10.1177/2167702617723376.

Social media is positively linked to depressive symptoms in high school students. More time spent on social media has also been shown to increase comparison, issues with self-confidence, and feelings of loneliness. Pantic, I. (2014). Online Social Networking and Mental Health. *Cyberpsychology, Behavior, And Social Networking, 17(10),* 652-657. doi: 10.1089/cyber.2014.0070. And Seabrook, EM, Kern, ML, & Rickard, NS (2016). Social Networking Sites, Depression, and Anxiety: A Systematic Review. *JMIR mental health, 3(4),* e50. doi:10.2196/mental.5842

Page 13: **It has become increasingly clear just how damaging device addiction is to their quality of learning and attention span**. And **Inattention lowers productivity and is yet another documented cost of unlimited connectivity.** The mere presence of one's phone consumes attention and working memory capacity even when it is not being checked. These effects are found when a phone is upside down, with no vibrations, silent on the desk compared to when it is in another room. *Ward, AF, Duke, K, Gneezy, A, & Bos, MW (2017). Brain drain: the mere presence of one's own smartphone reduces available cognitive capacity. Journal of the Association for Consumer Research,*(https://bit.ly/2C39PX3) *2(2),*

140–154. In a second study, participants reported higher levels of inattention and hyperactivity when alerts were on than when alerts were off. Higher levels of inattention in turn predicted lower productivity and psychological well-being. These findings highlight some of the costs of ubiquitous connectivity and suggest that people can reduce these costs simply by adjusting existing phone settings or by leaving their phones in other rooms. Kushlev, K, Proux, J, & Dunn, EW (2016) Silence Your Phones: Smartphone Notifications Increase Inattention and Hyperactivity Symptoms. *In Proceedings of the 2016 CHI Conference on Human Factors in Computing Systems (1011–1020) ACM.*

According to a survey conducted by Common Sense Media SurveyMonkey online poll conducted January 25 -29, 2018. https://www.commonsensemedia.org

Chapter 1:

Andy Nguyen explains that the happy chemical 'serotonin' kicks into our brain when we feel wanted, important and proud. Nguyen, A (2015) Hacking Your Happy Chemicals: Dopamine, Serotonin, Endorphins, & Oxytocin'. *The Utopian Life. N.p.,* 14 Oct. 2014. <http://www.huffingtonpost.com/thai-nguyen/hacking-into-your-happy-c_b_6007660.html>

Smart phones feed the human desire to be 'seen, heard, thought about, and monitored by others'. Quote found on page 2: Veissière, SP, & Stendel, M (2018). Hypernatural monitoring: a social rehearsal account of smartphone addiction. *Frontiers in psychology, 9,* 141. https://doi.org/10.3389/fpsyg.2018.00141

Page 15: **Dopamine, another significant 'feel good' chemical, is also responsible for giving us a high, and plays an important role in smartphone addiction**. Veissière, SP, & Stendel, M (2018). Hypernatural monitoring: a social rehearsal account of smartphone addiction. *Frontiers in psychology, 9,* 141. https://doi.org/10.3389/fpsyg.2018.00141

Page 16: **Delta FosB is a regulatory protein ...** Robison, AJ, & Nestler, EJ (2011). Transcriptional and epigenetic mechanisms of addiction. *Nature reviews neuroscience, 12(11),* 623.

Page 16: **There is an argument that teenagers are even more vulnerable...** Gillespie, D (2019) *Teen brain: Why screens are making your teenager depressed, anxious and prone to lifelong addictive illnesses – and how to stop it.* Pan Macmillan: Australia.

Page 16: **Two experiments demonstrated that people had poorer working memory and fluid intelligence when**

their phone was near. Ward, AF, Duke, K, Gneezy, A, & Bos, MW (2017). Brain drain: the mere presence of one's own smartphone reduces available cognitive capacity. *Journal of the Association for Consumer Research, 2*(2), 140–154.

Chapter 2

Part A: The Value of Being Connected

Page 19: **As humans, our social standing is enhanced when we are connected with what is happening in the world around us ... Quite simply, we are better off when we are switched on and know what is going on.** *Veissière, SP, & Stendel, M (2018). Hypernatural monitoring: a social rehearsal account of smartphone addiction. Frontiers in psychology, 9, 141. https://doi.org/10.3389/fpsyg.2018.00141*

Page 20: **We also are susceptible to a human desire to be thought about, seen, heard, guided and monitored by others.** This point is repeated from Chapter 1 (see reference provided above).

Page 20: **Dr Michael Carr-Gregg** suggested that we need to provide eight minutes per day with every child (on their own) giving them the attention they need. *Bita, N. Kids are sponges for bad parenting, 20th April 2016, The Australian.*

Page 20: **In unpublished research that we are currently conducting at Macquarie University, we've seen...** This refers to research being conducted through the Department of Psychology at Macquarie University. The people that have supported this research project are referred to in the acknowledgments.

Page 20: **Part B: Getting reassurance for every doubt**

Whether it be texting our worries to friends or using Google the moment a question crosses our minds, smartphones provide reassurance for every doubt. Unfortunately, a negative side effect of this instant world is growing impatience, and the undermining of our willingness to wait to find things out. Multiple studies have shown that people who express a stronger need to know what the future will bring are more likely to display a greater number of simultaneous psychological difficulties than people who are more relaxed with knowing what the future will bring. McEvoy, PM, & Mahoney, AE (2012). To be sure, to be sure: Intolerance of uncertainty mediates symptoms of various anxiety disorders and depression. *Behavior therapy, 43(3),* 533–545.

Page 22: **Part D: Envy**

Sometimes we feel worse rather than better when scrolling through our social media feeds.

Kross, E, Verduyn, P, Demiralp, E, Park, J, Lee, DS, Lin, N, ... & Ybarra, O (2013). Facebook use predicts declines in subjective well-being in young adults. *PloS one, 8(8),* e69841; Tandoc, Edson C., Patrick Ferrucci, and Margaret Duffy. (2015) Facebook use, envy, and depression among college students: Is Facebooking depressing? *Computers in Human Behavior, 43,* 139–146.

Page 23: **Studies have shown that constant social media contact is associated with loneliness and self-confidence issues, with more than three hours of screen time per day being associated with depression and suicidal outcomes.** The author notes for these comments are given in the introduction (see above p97).

Chapter 4

Page 37: **The current recommendation by the <u>Office of the E-safety Commissioner</u>** (https://bit.ly/2WH0wIx) **for children** between the ages of 5 and 17 years is less than two hours per day for non-educational use. Two US surveys based on 506,820 teenagers indicated that those who spent more time on social media and smartphones were more likely to report mental health issues (in particular, depressive symptoms) than those who spent more time on non-screen activities. In that research paper the concerning risks were described as 'constant social media use' and 'over 3 hours' per day reported on screens. As cited in Introduction Notes. Twenge *et al*, 2018, see above p97)

Chapter 5

Page 45: **According to a 2013 US survey some.... per day with screen media.** Wartella, E., Rideout, V., Lauricella, A. R., & Connell, S. (2013). Parenting in the age of digital technology. Report for the center on media and Human development school of communication Northwestern University.

Page 47: **Research shows that although comprehension is not impaired, recall is poorer from multitasking.** Glass and Kang (2019), Dividing attention in the classroom reduces exam performance. *Educational Psychology, 39 (3),* 395-408. https://www.tandfonline.com/doi/full/10.1080/01443410.2018.1489046

Page 48: **Take a moment to consider whether to reward .... your child will view reading as a 'task' and be less likely to persist.** Deci, E. L., Koestner, R., & Ryan, R. M. (1999). A meta-analytic review of experiments examining the effects of extrinsic rewards on intrinsic motivation. *Psychological Bulletin, 125,* 627-668.

Page 56: **Talk to your child about the importance of building strength.** Waters, L. E. (2015). Strength-based parenting and life satisfaction in teenagers. *Advances in Social Sciences Research Journal, 2*(11). Waters, L. (2017). *The strength switch: How the new science of strength-based parenting can help your child and your teen to flourish.* Penguin.

Page 56: **Creative tasks distract us from worries, build confidence and provide space to work through problems encountered in everyday life.** There is an excellent survey (https:// bit.ly/2DXEAOM) being offered in the UK to stimulate creative activities for those over 18 years. It provides a personalised Feel Good Formula and stimulates ideas worth considering.

A comment on Smart-Watches

Page 59: Please see author note The mere presence of one's phone consumes attention and working memory capacity even when it is not being checked. These effects are found when a phone is upside down, with no vibrations, silent on the desk compared to when it is in another room. Ward, AF, Duke, K, Gneezy, A, & Bos, MW (2017). Brain drain: the mere presence of one's own smartphone reduces available cognitive capacity. Journal of the Association for Consumer Research, 2(2), 140–154. And Einstein, DA (2017) Anxiety and uncertainty in the age of the smartphone — and what we can do about it. The Conversation. https://www.abc.net.au/news/2017-10-25/ smartphonedealing-with-uncertainty-andanxiety-in-digital-age/9085194

ACKNOWLEDGEMENTS

I would like to acknowledge my friends for supporting the development of this book. I am indebted to:

Monique van Tulder, the Urban Mum(https://bit.ly/2WRj9db), for sparking the idea, and Mark Hadassin, my husband, for providing a different sort of inspiration… in addition to his ongoing patience and support.

Debbie Kertesz, founder of HumanKind (https://bit.ly/2H-SIz1n), for constructive feedback.

Joe Hadassin, who is competent, capable and always helps me; and Sam Hadassin, who is crafty, clever and featured in the first video—there wouldn't be a book without you two!

Peter Butchart and Judy Koenig, from Perisher Huette, for wordsmithing, encouragement, and up-to-date insights into relevant media coverage.

Yael Barnett, Judith Einstein, Amanda Redhill, Hayley Leib, David Einstein, Lindi Greenfield, Janina Nearn, Kate Riley-Sandler, Rowena Young and Brett Sandler for their insights.

Annabel Bennett and Lyria Bennett Moses for stepping in with sideline mentoring and support (as always).

Kaz Williams from Big Shed Creative for her generous advice, Emily Little for her research assistance and thoughtful contribution, Russell Thomson for editing the book and Lauren Finger for facilitating the project.

I am indebted to the following people who have provided support on the research that I lead as an Adjunct Fellow at Macquarie University. These include Miriam Capper, Research Assistant, and the following collaborators: Dr Anne McMaugh, Professor Peter McEvoy, Professor Ron Rapee, Associate Professor Maree Abbott, Dr Madeleine Ferrari and Dr Eyal Karin, as well as the amazing group of teachers and school counselors from six secondary schools including in particular Mrs Melissa Boyd, Mr Sinclair Watson, Ms Therese O'Neill, Ms Lorraine Cushing, Mrs Claire Melloy and Mr David Heath for their thoughtful contribution to this project.

Dedicated to my Mum, Judith, who has patiently given up her life to support my Dad, Clifford.

About the Author

Dr Danielle Einstein has 23 years' experience as a Clinical Psychologist, including working as Director of her own private practice, Distinct Psychology, since 2003. She commenced her career as Head of the Anxiety Clinic at Westmead Hospital and has published international peer reviewed papers in the areas of anxiety, depression and obsessive compulsive disorder. Danielle currently conducts research as an Adjunct Fellow with Macquarie University developing novel interventions to prevent anxiety and depression. She works with schools on wellbeing programs that teach smart technology use to enhance emotional health. Danielle has led the development of many school based programs, including EMI, Insights and the Dip@School Program.